LIVERPOOL

RIVER MERSEY

THE BEATLES' LIVERPOOL

T0002468

INTRODUCTION

Liverpool sits on the bank of the River Mersey in north-west England. Whatever your interests it is a wonderful, exciting and historic city to visit, boasting as it does a wealth of shops, cafés, restaurants, theatres, art galleries and an array of internationally impressive museums.

Liverpool is also home to two of the UK's greatest ever football teams. It has given the world magnificent actors including Tom Baker, Kim Cattrall, Jason Isaacs, Jodie Comer and the McGann brothers. Liverpool humour has been exported to the world by the likes of Tommy Handley, Arthur Askey, Ken Dodd, Jimmy Tarbuck, Alexei Sayle and John Bishop. And, of course, the city boasts an array of iconic architecture. This includes the buildings known as the Three Graces, which dominate the riverside skyline, with the Liver Birds themselves sitting atop the Royal Liver Building.

And yet in the whole history of the city there is perhaps one group of Liverpudlians who changed the world more than any other.

The Beatles – John Lennon, Paul McCartney, George Harrison and Ringo Starr – were all born and brought up here in Merseyside. This is where their parents and wider families lived, where they received their education and where they met their first girlfriends. They first met each other, discovered music and learned to sing and play in this city. It was in the music shops of Liverpool that they bought their first instruments. Their manager Brian Epstein was also born here and this is where he established his NEMS organisation and signed them. The Cavern and Casbah Clubs, as well as the scores of other halls and venues where they learned their craft and built up their fanbase through the early years, are also all spread across Merseyside. And, of course, the places they celebrated in song, such as Strawberry Fields and Penny Lane, are now Liverpool landmarks.

The aim of this book, therefore, is to provide you with an introduction and guide to the significant locations associated with The Beatles' early career, locations that are spread across the great city of Liverpool and the wider Merseyside area. This, then, is Beatle Land, the place that produced the greatest act in popular music history.

LEFT Premiere of *A Hard Day's Night*. Crowds gather to catch sight of The Beatles before the northern premiere starts in Liverpool, 10 July 1964.

1. THE PIER HEAD

The Pier Head is the location of the buildings known as the Three Graces, which look over the River Mersey and form one of Liverpool's most recognisable architectural sites. Conceived as visible symbols of the city's maritime heritage, they are, from left to right: the Royal Liver Building (opened in 1911 as the home of the Royal Liver Assurance friendly society), the Cunard Building (opened in 1917 as the headquarters of the Cunard shipping line) and the Port of Liverpool Building (the offices of the Mersey Docks and Harbour Board, opened in 1907). And just in front of Liverpool's three most famous buildings stands a statue celebrating four of its most famous sons.

The 8-foot tall Beatles statue was commissioned by the current owners of the Cavern Club and erected in 2015. The sculpture is based on a 1963 photograph of the then newly famous band and presents the boys in the order they appeared on stage. Paul and George are to the left, Ringo is slightly behind the others in the middle and John strides forward on the right.

Each of the figures also carries their own distinctive feature. George has an Indian mantra on his belt, Ringo has L8, the postal area of Liverpool in which he grew up, on his shoe, Paul carries a camera bag in tribute to his photographer wife Linda, and John holds a pair of acorns, symbolising those that he and his wife Yoko Ono sent to world leaders in 1969 to promote world peace.

LEFT The iconic buildings known as the Three Graces overlooking the River Mersey.

BELOW The Beatles statue on Liverpool's Waterfront.

2. THE MERSEY FERRY

The famous Ferry across the Mersey was, of course, celebrated in song by The Beatles' friends, contemporaries and record-label mates Gerry and the Pacemakers. You can still take the Mersey ferry today to cross the river to Birkenhead or Seacombe in the Wirral.

The route to Birkenhead was first provided from 1150, when monks from Birkenhead Priory would row passengers across the river. In 1815, steam vessels were introduced and during the First World War the Mersey ferry boats *Iris* and *Daffodil* played a significant role in a raid on Zeebrugge. Following this, King George V granted the boats permission to use 'Royal' as part of their names.

The Beatles played on board the *Royal Iris* several times in their early days. The *Royal Iris* was equipped with bars and even a fish and chip counter, which led to her being known as 'the floating fish and chip shop'. It was therefore the perfect setting for evening cruise events such as The Riverboat Shuffles, which were held in 1961 and 1962, featuring The Beatles alongside other musical acts ranging from trad jazz star Acker Bilk to rockers Johnny Kidd & the Pirates.

The Liverpool boats' role in the Great War was further commemorated in 2015 when another of the ferry fleet, *Snowdrop*, was repainted with a special new design. This dazzle ship style pattern was inspired by the

technique used to camouflage warships in the First World War and was created by none other than Sir Peter Blake, who famously provided the cover for The Beatles' 1967 LP *Sgt. Pepper's Lonely Hearts Club Band*. Blake's work, entitled *Everybody Razzle Dazzle*, now serves as a floating piece of art on the River Mersey, connecting the ferries' historic war service with Liverpool's greatest musical export.

ABOVE John, Paul, George and Ringo on board the Mersey Ferry during filming of the BBC TV documentary *The Mersey Sound* in August 1963.

LEFT The Mersey ferryboat *Snowdrop*, painted with the dazzle ship design created by Sir Peter Blake.

3. THE ROYAL ALBERT DOCK

A short distance from the Pier Head is the Royal Albert Dock, constructed in 1846. Having been built without structural wood, the Albert Dock was the first non-combustible warehouse in the world. In the 1980s, it was converted into an area of shops, restaurants, bars and museums.

The attractions around the Royal Albert Dock include the Merseyside Maritime Museum, Tate Liverpool and, of course, *The Beatles Story*, the world's largest permanent exhibition of the lives and times of The Beatles. Exhibits here include not only original instruments, clothing, artwork and memorabilia, but handwritten lyrics and even a pair of John's glasses!

4. QUEEN VICTORIA MONUMENT

The statue of Queen Victoria in Derby Square marks the site where Liverpool Castle was erected c.1230 to protect the new port of Liverpool, which King John had called into existence by means of a royal charter in 1207.

The monument was also the location around which The Beatles were photographed in 1963. A few years earlier in May 1958, their future manager Brian Epstein came here to pay off a man who was blackmailing him following a gay sexual encounter. After taking the money the blackmailer was arrested by police, whose involvement had been negotiated by Brian's solicitor.

ABOVE The Royal Albert Dock.

TOP The Beatles photographed on the Queen Victoria Monument in February 1963.

5. NEMS

Brian Epstein's NEMS shop and offices first opened their doors on 31 May 1960, at the corner of Whitechapel and the city's main traditional shopping area Church Street.

Brian's grandfather Isaac had established the family's original Liverpool shop selling furniture on Walton Road in the north of the city. In 1929, Isaac had bought up a neighbouring business called North End Road Music Stores and in 1957 the Epsteins opened a NEMS store in the city centre on Great Charlotte Street. Brian was responsible for the shop's record department and this proved so successful that the Whitechapel premises were opened in 1960 with Brian as manager.

Brian prided himself on being able to provide any record requested by customers and even knew their catalogue numbers by heart. The local music paper *Mersey Beat* was sold in the shop from its first issue on 6 July 1961 (coincidentally the fourth anniversary of Paul and John's meeting at the Woolton fete) and Brian began contributing a column from the third issue on 3 August.

On 28 October 1961, a scruffy, leather-clad young boy called Raymond Jones walked into NEMS on Whitechapel and asked for a copy of 'My Bonnie', the single recorded by The Beatles with singer Tony Sheridan for Polydor in Germany. When his staff were unable to find any details for the disc, Brian's interest was piqued and he determined to find out more about this local band about whom, he claimed, he had not previously heard.

It was therefore from NEMS' premises on Whitechapel that Brian and his assistant Alistair Taylor set out on 9 November 1961 to go and see The Beatles for themselves at a lunchtime session at The Cavern. They crossed Whitechapel then turned left up Button Street before walking through Rainford Gardens and into Mathew Street.

ABOVE LEFT Brian Epstein's Whitechapel NEMS shop and offices in their heyday.

TOP The junction of Whitechapel with Church Street and Lord Street, where NEMS was once located.

ABOVE Brian Epstein would have crossed Whitechapel and turned up Button Street on his historic walk to see The Beatles at The Cavern for the first time.

On the way they passed the White Star and Grapes pubs, which were frequented by The Beatles and other performers, eventually reaching The Cavern at 10 Mathew Street. This walk, which changed Brian and The Beatles' lives as well as that of popular music history, would probably have taken only around three minutes.

The Beatles, including drummer Pete Best, signed a contract with Brian at the NEMS offices on 24 January 1962. It was also here in August 1962 that Brian had the job of informing Pete that he was out of the band and where John, Paul, George and Ringo signed a new contract on 1 October.

The Whitechapel offices became the nerve centre for the many Merseybeat artists managed by Brian, who included The Beatles, Gerry and the Pacemakers, Billy J. Kramer & the Dakotas, The Fourmost and Cilla Black. The growth of the NEMS empire soon led to the business moving a short distance away to Moorfields in the summer of 1963.

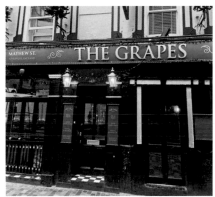

LEFT The Beatles were regulars at the White Star on Rainford Gardens, which Brian Epstein would have passed on his way to Mathew Street and The Cavern.

BELOW LEFT The Grapes public house on Mathew Street, which was also frequented by The Beatles and other Merseybeat bands in between sessions at The Cavern.

6. CILLA BLACK STATUE

Just outside The Cavern stands a statue to The Beatles' great friend and contemporary Cilla Black. Cilla worked in The Cavern's cloakroom as well as appearing on stage in her own right as a singer, occasionally with The Beatles as her backing band. She of course went on to become a legendary figure on British television.

Another artwork on the wall opposite The Cavern entrance was created by the great Liverpool sculptor Arthur Dooley and is simply but powerfully titled *Four Lads Who Shook The World*. Across Mathew Street The Liverpool Beatles Museum stands next to The Grapes pub.

ABOVE Arthur Dooley's 1974 sculpture *Four Lads Who Shook The World*.

LEFT The statue of Cilla Black welcomes visitors to The Cavern, where she once worked and sang.

7. THE CAVERN

The Cavern Club was established by Alan Sytner, who lived with his parents on Menlove Avenue (a little way along from John Lennon's home with his Aunt Mimi). After a visit to Paris where he saw the basement jazz club Le Caveau de la Huchette, Sytner was inspired to open his own venue. He found a basement site on Mathew Street, which he said reminded him of the narrow streets of Paris' Left Bank and opened The Cavern here in January 1957 as a jazz club.

At this time, Mathew Street would have been a dark, unwelcoming place, lined on each side with tall warehouses. The only way in or out of The Cavern was down 18 very narrow stone steps which took you below street level into a former fruit warehouse measuring 58 by 39 feet. The maximum number of people ever in the club at one time was 652, although around 2,000 were said to have turned up wanting to get in on the first night to see the Merseysippi Jazz Band.

The Cavern was dark, dingy, smelly and damp. If you touched the stone walls your hand would come away wet. Cloakrooms and a small bar stood in the arches along one side of the cellar. At the end of the room the stage was built into one of the arches. Because of the low ceiling, performers on stage had very little headroom.

The carpenters who constructed the stage were in fact Paul McCartney's cousin Ian Harris and his dad Harry (the husband of Paul's Auntie Jin who is name-checked in the 1976 Wings hit 'Let 'Em In'). The Quarrymen first played here soon after the club opened, as did Ringo as a member of the Eddie Clayton Skiffle Group. Paul first played here with The Quarrymen in early 1958. Although rock and roll was frowned upon by jazz enthusiasts, skiffle was tolerated as it had developed out of breakout sessions performed during trad jazz performances. From 1960 however, the club began hosting beat groups with lunchtime sessions held to entertain local office and shop workers.

The Beatles (John, Paul, George and their early drummer Pete Best) first appeared here

BELOW LEFT The Cavern entrance on Mathew Street.

BELOW The stage of the modern-day Cavern Club.

at a lunchtime show on 9 February 1961 and were paid £5 for their trouble. From 6 March 1961, they began appearing more frequently both at lunchtime and evening sessions.

Brian Epstein first saw them perform here at lunchtime on 9 November 1961 and said, 'It was very interesting to see all of these teenagers spending their lunch hour in rapt attention to these rather scruffy lads on stage.' His assistant Alistair Taylor described 'this very scruffy band on stage in black leather and black T-shirts. They were fooling about and they weren't very good musicians. But it was the most phenomenal experience I've ever gone through. They were incredible! . . . You could literally feel the sound hitting you, pounding against your chest.'

Following Pete Best's dismissal, Ringo first appeared here with The Beatles on 22 August 1962, when they were filmed by Granada Television performing 'Some Other Guy'.

The Beatles made their final appearance at The Cavern in August 1963, by which time they had already topped the UK charts with

'From Me To You' and were about to release 'She Loves You'.

The Cavern also played host to all the other legendary local acts, including Gerry and the Pacemakers, The Searchers, The Big Three, Billy J. Kramer & the Dakotas, The Undertakers, The Mojos, The Merseybeats and – of course – Cilla Black.

In later years bands including The Rolling Stones, The Kinks, The Who, Status Quo and Queen all took to the stage here, but in 1973 the venue was closed and filled in to build a ventilation shaft for the Merseyrail underground system. The venue moved across the road to a new site, which in 1976 became the home of Eric's, a venue that provided a home to a new generation of great Liverpool bands including Echo and the Bunnymen, The Teardrop Explodes, Wah! Heat, Big in Japan, Deaf School and Orchestral Manoeuvres in the Dark.

In the early 1980s, however, The Cavern was reconstructed and reopened back at its original address on Mathew Street.

ABOVE Outside The Cavern stands Arthur Dooley's statue inspired by a famous photo taken of John Lennon in Hamburg.

LEFT The *Eleanor Rigby* statue is on Stanley Street near the site of Frank Hessy's shop. It was sculpted in 1982 by early British rock and roll star Tommy Steele.

ABOVE A plaque now marks the site on Stanley Street where Frank Hessy's shop once stood.

8. FRANK HESSY'S MUSIC CENTRE

Although now a somewhat unprepossessing shop site, 62 Stanley Street was from 1959 the home of Frank Hessy's Music Centre, where The Quarrymen and then The Beatles bought their first guitars. Hessy's dealt largely in second-hand instruments and was thus frequented not only by John, Paul, George and friends, but by budding cash-strapped Liverpool musicians through many decades.

In July 1957, Paul McCartney visited Hessy's earlier store on Manchester Street to trade in a trumpet his dad had bought him in exchange for his first guitar, a £15 Zenith F hole. In August 1959, John Lennon purchased his first half-decent guitar here, a Hofner Club 40, and in November 1959, George Harrison also visited Hessy's to buy the Delicia Futurama guitar, which he used over the next few years. George said the Futurama had a great sound but was 'a dog to play'!

In 1960, John Lennon persuaded his art college friend Stuart Sutcliffe to come to Hessy's to buy a Hofner President bass guitar and amplifier with the money he had recently received from the sale of a painting. Stuart then had to learn to play the instrument from scratch to become The Beatles' first bassist. Paul was also back again at Hessy's that year to buy himself a Rosetti Solid 7 guitar.

Paul has also said that it was Hessy's chief salesman Jim Gretty who taught him to play the F7#9 guitar chord, which was used in songs such as 'Michelle' and 'Taxman'.

9. RUSHWORTH AND DREAPER

Rushworth and Dreaper's music store stood at 42 Whitechapel. In 1962, John and George were photographed here picking up a pair of brand-new sunburst Gibson J-160E acoustic guitars, which had been imported specially from the US at a cost of £161 each. This must have seemed an extraordinary price as the average annual salary in the UK at that time was £779. John and George used their new guitars the very next day on the album recording of 'Love Me Do'.

LEFT John and George being presented with their specially ordered Gibson J-160E guitars at Rushworth and Dreaper in September 1962.

10. THE EMPIRE THEATRE

Liverpool's Empire Theatre opened in 1925 and, with 2,350 seats, is Britain's largest two-tier auditorium. In June 1957, John Lennon's band The Quarrymen appeared on stage at the Empire to perform an audition for Carroll Levis and his television talent contest show *TV Star Search*. Unfortunately they did not pass the audition on this occasion and so did not get to appear on television.

The Beatles first appeared here following the release of their debut single 'Love Me Do' in October 1962. They returned to the Empire several times as their national and international fame grew over the next few years and made their final ever live appearances in Liverpool here in late 1965. The Empire is therefore the location of one of The Quarrymen's first performances and also The Beatles' last in the city.

Opposite the Empire is one of Liverpool's most iconic areas, including the magnificent St George's Hall and William Brown Street, which houses the city's central library, the World Museum and the Walker Art Gallery. St George's Hall opened in 1854 to provide a setting for concerts, meetings and dinners, as well as a home for Liverpool's law courts. Early Beatles manager Allan Williams recalled hiring the hall in 1959 for an arts ball and got John Lennon and Stuart Sutcliffe to make ornate floats for the event, which they did with help from Paul McCartney and George Harrison. Stuart became very dejected after the crowd destroyed the floats as was traditional at such an event.

ABOVE The Empire Theatre stands on Lime Street next to Liverpool's main railway station and opposite St George's Hall.

BELOW 38 Kensington, where The Quarrymen paid to cut their recording of 'That'll Be The Day'.

11. 38 KENSINGTON

In their pre-Beatle days John, Paul, George and their fellow Quarrymen came to this terraced house about a mile beyond the city centre to record their first ever disc. The owner Percy Phillips had set up a recording studio where budding musicians such as The Quarrymen could pay around 17 shillings and sixpence (about 88p) to record two songs straight to an acetate disc. The songs recorded during The Quarrymen session were Buddy Holly's 'That'll Be The Day' and 'In Spite of All The Danger', the only song ever credited to Paul McCartney and George Harrison together. The group took it in turns to look after the single copy of the record that they took away, although pianist John Lowe ended up keeping it for 23 years. In 2005, John Lowe and drummer Colin Hanton unveiled a blue plaque on the house to commemorate the event.

12. LIVERPOOL COLLEGE OF ART

Liverpool College of Art, the art school attended by John Lennon and Stuart Sutcliffe, stood at 68 Hope Street. It was here that the 16-year-old John Lennon enrolled as a student on 16 September 1957 to study for a National Diploma in Art and Design, a course covering the history of art, ceramics and lettering. John had come from Quarry Bank School, as had another student two years his senior, Bill Harry. Bill would go on to found and edit the *Mersey Beat* music paper while attending the Art College and it was Bill who introduced John to the college's most talented student, Stuart Sutcliffe. It was also at the college that John met his future wife Cynthia Powell. Cynthia began at the college in the same year as John

and, although they were not in the same work group, they did cross paths for classes such as Lettering. John teased Cynthia for coming from the supposedly genteel Wirral, but it turned out they had something in common – the pair were almost as exactly short-sighted as one another! At lunchtime one day late in 1958, John asked Cynthia to dance to a song being played on the gramophone. She protested that she was engaged to a boy in Hoylake. 'I didn't ask you to ****in' marry me did I?' responded Lennon. John then asked Cynthia for an afternoon drink at the nearby pub Ye Cracke and sure enough the couple were soon going out together.

BELOW The site of Liverpool College of Art on Hope Street with *A Case History*, a sculpture unveiled in 1998 featuring suitcases labelled with the names of famous owners from Liverpool.

14　THE BEATLES' LIVERPOOL

13. LIVERPOOL INSTITUTE

Now the Liverpool Institute of Performing Arts, this was once the secondary school attended by Paul McCartney and George Harrison. The Liverpool Institute High School for Boys or, as it was popularly known, The Inny, stood immediately adjacent to the Liverpool College of Art. This school, managed by Liverpool City Council, opened in 1905 and eventually closed in 1985.

The 11-year-old Paul McCartney started here as a pupil in class 3c in 1953, followed by George Harrison a year later in 1954. It was also at the Inny that Paul became friends with a classmate called Ivan Vaughan with whom he shared the same birthday. It would be Ivan who, a few years later, would introduce him to John Lennon, at the Woolton fete. Another pupil in 3c was Neil Aspinall, who would go on to be The Beatles' road manager and eventually Chief Executive of Apple. George Harrison was a pupil at the Inny until 1959,

but Paul stayed on into the sixth form. Paul did his A Level exams in 1960, despite having had to take a week off school in May in order to tour Scotland with The Beatles backing singer Johnny Gentle.

ABOVE Paul McCartney's LIPA school, which now occupies the building that formerly housed his secondary school, the Liverpool Institute High School for Boys.

14. LIVERPOOL MATERNITY HOSPITAL

The Liverpool Maternity Hospital was opened in March 1924 and today has been converted to provide student accommodation for Liverpool University. It was here in the second-floor ward on 9 October 1940 that Julia Lennon gave birth to John. Her sister, John's Aunt Mimi, claimed he was born during an air raid and she had had to hide in doorways on her way to the hospital to avoid shrapnel, but in fact there were no bombing raids on Liverpool on the night of John's birth.

LEFT & ABOVE The old Liverpool Maternity Hospital building on Cambridge Court off Oxford Street and the plaque by the door commemorating John Lennon's birth here.

LEFT Beatles manager Brian Epstein with John Lennon.

BELOW LEFT Brian Epstein's birthplace on Rodney Street.

16. 197 QUEENS DRIVE

The Epstein family home was on Queens Drive a few miles north-east of the city. Brian and his brother Clive lived with their parents Harry and Queenie in a comfortable and relatively substantial detached home. This property had been bought thanks to the profits from the Epstein family business, originally established by Harry's father Isaac and which, of course, Brian and Clive would ultimately take over and manage under the name NEMS.

15. 4 RODNEY STREET

Beatles manager Brian Epstein was born at 4 Rodney Street on Yom Kippur, 19 September 1934 to Harry and Malka (aka Queenie) Epstein, who had married the year before. The address where Brian was born was not, however, their family home but a private nursing home. Rodney Street stands in what is now known as Liverpool's Georgian Quarter, a prestigious area just east of the city centre which was built during the expansion of Liverpool in the late 18th century. British Prime Minister William Gladstone was born at 62 Rodney Street in 1809.

ABOVE The family home Brian Epstein shared with his parents and his brother Clive on Queens Drive near Childwall.

LEFT Brian Epstein's grave in the Long Lane Jewish Cemetery.

17. LIVERPOOL JEWISH CEMETERY

Brian Epstein died on 27 August 1967 at his home on Chapel Street, Belgravia. His body was returned to Liverpool and buried in the Long Lane Jewish Cemetery in the north-east of the city.

RIGHT Allan Williams' Jacaranda club on Slater Street and the site from which The Beatles set off for their trip to Hamburg in August 1960.

18. THE JACARANDA

Allan Williams opened the Jacaranda at 21 Slater Street in September 1958. On street level the Jac offered a café providing food and frothy coffee and became popular with students from the nearby College of Art. In the basement there was a music venue with a tiny dance floor where the resident band was the Royal Caribbean Steel Band fronted by Allan's friend Harold Phillips, better known as Lord Woodbine. Two students from the art school, Stuart Sutcliffe and Rod Murray, helped decorate the basement while Allan claimed that the ladies' toilets had been decorated by Stuart and John Lennon!

In 1960, the newly named Beatles began rehearsing and performing at The Jacaranda. Allan Williams arranged their audition with impresario Larry Parnes, which resulted in their touring Scotland in May 1960 as backing band for singer Johnny Gentle. A few months later Williams also set up the band's first engagement in Hamburg from August to December 1960. As they were lacking a drummer for the Hamburg booking, Pete Best came here to audition on 15 August 1960. The next day Allan drove his friend Lord Woodbine, his wife Beryl and her brother Barry Chang as well as John, Paul, George, Stuart and their newly appointed drummer Pete all the way to Hamburg. The group set off by van for this life-changing trip from just outside the club.

19. 64 MOUNT PLEASANT

John and Cynthia Lennon were married on 23 August 1962 at the Liverpool Register Office, which at the time was located at 64 Mount Pleasant. Cynthia had recently discovered she was pregnant with their child Julian, who would be born the following April. Famously John's response to the news was: 'There's only one thing for it Cyn – we'll have to get married.'

Beatles manager Brian Epstein acted as John's best man while Paul and George were also present. Ringo was not at the wedding having only just played his first show with them a few days before.

ABOVE 64 Mount Pleasant, where John Lennon and Cynthia Powell were married in August 1962.

20. YE CRACKE

Ye Cracke is a small pub situated at 13 Rice Street, a short distance from the art college attended by John Lennon. It was therefore a handy and popular destination for John and his fellow students, including his girlfriend Cynthia, Stuart Sutcliffe, Rod Murray and *Mersey Beat* newspaper founder Bill Harry. Indeed it was at Ye Cracke that Harry first introduced John to Stuart and it was where John first invited Cynthia for a drink in late 1958. John also came here with his other art school friend Jeff Mohammed and sat in the rear bar below an etching depicting the death of Nelson. The drawing showed the great naval hero surrounded by his aghast and horrified-looking crew, so John captioned it: 'Who farted?'

John's preferred drink at Ye Cracke is said to have been Black Velvet, a cocktail made from Guinness and sparkling wine. An artwork on the wall of the bar commemorates John, Stuart, Rod Murray and Bill Harry as The Dissenters. The four came to Ye Cracke after attending a June 1960 reading by British beat poet Royston Ellis. They are said to have been unimpressed by his performance and decided instead to put Liverpool on the map in their own individual way.

ABOVE The Beatles peering out from behind their dressing room door before their appearance at the Odeon Theatre in Manchester, 30 May 1963.

RIGHT Ye Cracke, one of John Lennon's favourite pubs while he was a student at the nearby College of Art.

21. 3 GAMBIER TERRACE

Gambier Terrace is a row of 19th-century houses overlooking Liverpool Cathedral. Stuart Sutcliffe and fellow art student Rod Murray were given notice at their previous flat nearby on Percy Street when their landlady discovered they had used a pile of antique furniture for firewood. They moved in to a large flat at Gambier Terrace where they were joined by fellow students Margaret Morris, Margaret Duxbury and John Lennon. John taught Stuart to play bass guitar here and the pair practised along with Paul and George. It was also here in this flat sometime early in 1960 that John and Stuart came up with the new name for their band: The Beatles.

The flat was reportedly filthy and its squalour even made it into the national newspapers. Following a meeting between Allan Williams and a couple of journalists in Ye Cracke, a piece headed 'This is the Beatnik Horror' appeared in the *Sunday People* newspaper extolling the filth and depravity in which British students were currently living. Williams was noticeable in the photographs accompanying the article and Rod Murray was named as a tenant, but neither Stuart nor John were mentioned.

As a result of the bad publicity the residents were given notice to quit. Luckily for John and Stuart the eviction coincided with their leaving to play in Hamburg with the rest of The Beatles in August 1960.

ABOVE Gambier Terrace, along Hope Street from the College of Art, where John Lennon and Stuart Sutcliffe lived in early 1960.

22. LIVERPOOL CATHEDRAL

Liverpool Cathedral stands on St James Mount opposite Gambier Terrace and was constructed mostly from sandstone from Woolton Quarry, John's home village. St James Mount was itself used as a quarry from the 16th century and provided stone for Liverpool's Old Dock and Town Hall. In 1827, part of the area was made into a cemetery for the city. Among those buried here are Liverpool MP William Huskisson who was run over by Stephenson's Rocket in 1830, during the Rainhill Railway trials held near the city.

As a boy Paul McCartney applied to be in the cathedral choir here (but sadly failed the audition); later in the 1950s he, John and George would 'sag off' school and college

to hang out in the cathedral grounds. Paul returned to the cathedral in rather different circumstances in 1991 when his first major classical work, the *Liverpool Oratorio*, was premiered here.

ABOVE Liverpool's Anglican cathedral, the largest religious building in Britain and the eighth largest church in the world.

23. DINGLE

Two miles south of Liverpool city centre is Dingle, a traditionally working-class area that takes its name from the Dingle Brook, a lost tributary of the Mersey that once ran through it. As the city sprawled outwards in the mid 19th century, Dingle became built up with terraced houses erected to home settlers from Wales moving into the area. For this reason many streets in the area have Welsh names.

Richard Starkey, aka Beatles drummer Ringo Starr, was born here in an upstairs room at 9 Madryn Street on 7 July 1940. His mum and dad, Richard and Elsie, were paying 14s 10d (64p) a week in rent for the property at the time. They split up when he was three years old and he moved with his mum to 10 Admiral Grove, a smaller house with an even lower rent, just a couple of minutes' walk away. Elsie took a job at The Empress pub round the corner from Admiral Grove and this building features on the cover of Ringo's first solo album *Sentimental Journey*, released in 1970.

RIngo's mum remarried and his step-dad Harry Graves bought him a set of drums when he was 16. Ringo's first band was the Eddie Clayton Skiffle Group, led by a friend and neighbour from Admiral Grove. In 1959 Ringo changed bands and became drummer with an act called The Raving Texans. This group would eventually become better known as Rory Storm and the Hurricanes, one of the most successful on the local scene in the early 1960s.

10 Admiral Grove remained Ringo's home until his career with The Beatles took off and in 1963, he moved Harry Graves and his mum to a house he had bought for them further out of the city in Gateacre.

ABOVE 10 Admiral Grove, Ringo Starr's home for much of his childhood.

RIGHT The Empress pub on High Park Street, Dingle, just around the corner from Admiral Grove.

RIGHT Ringo Starr
pictured leaving his
family home in Admiral
Grove, Liverpool,
7 December 1963.
Ringo was on his way
to the Empire Theatre,
where a special edition
of the BBC television
show *Juke Box Jury*
would be filmed.

24. ROYAL LIVERPOOL CHILDREN'S HOSPITAL

Ringo's early life in Dingle was interrupted
when he developed peritonitis after his
appendix ruptured in 1946, leading to a
12-month stay in hospital in Liverpool.

Seven years later he contracted pleurisy
and this time spent two years in hospital, first
in Liverpool and then in the Royal Liverpool
Children's Hospital, which was in fact located
across the Mersey in Heswall, Wirral. It was
during this second stay in hospital that Ringo
found his love for drumming as a result of
percussion sessions held on his ward to
entertain the children.

ABOVE The Royal Liverpool Children's Hospital stood
on Telegraph Road, Heswall, until its closure in 1985,
after which it was demolished.

25. SEFTON PARK

Heading south out of Liverpool through Toxteth and Dingle brings you to two large municipal parks, Prince's Park and Sefton Park.

Prince's Park was named after Queen Victoria's son, Prince Edward (the future Edward VII) who was born the year it opened in 1842. Sefton Park was opened 30 years later on land purchased by Liverpool corporation from the Earl of Sefton. These parks would have been known to all The Beatles in their youth. Indeed Ringo is said to have lost his virginity in Sefton Park in 1957 with a girl he had just met at a funfair!

In 1928 John Lennon's parents first met in Sefton Park when the then 14-year-old Julia Stanley told 15-year-old Alf Lennon that the bowler hat he was wearing looked silly. When Alf took his hat off, Julia snatched it and threw it into the large lake that sits in the centre of the park. The couple eventually married in December 1938.

Sefton Park also boasts a magnificent three-tiered dome palm house. The Palm House first opened in 1896 but its glass was entirely shattered during World War II when a bomb fell close to the park. Today the Palm House has been restored following a campaign in the 1990s. Nearby stands Sefton Park's bandstand with its pagoda-style roof. This also dates from Victorian times and is claimed to have provided The Beatles with the inspiration for their *Sgt. Pepper* cover image.

LEFT Aerial view of Sefton Park showing the Palm House and the edge of the lake.

26. STUART SUTCLIFFE'S HOMES

Two houses occupied at different times by early Beatles bassist Stuart Sutcliffe and his family stand on opposite sides of Sefton Park.

In 1960, the Sutcliffes moved to Ullet Road to the north of the park. It would have been to this address that Stuart returned home after The Beatles' performance at Lathom Hall, Seaforth in January 1961. A group of local teddy boys had cornered Stuart after this show and given him a bad beating, which some say may have contributed to his fatal brain haemorrhage a year later.

In 1961 the Sutcliffes moved across the park to 37 Aigburth Drive, today known as the Sefton Park Hotel. Following The Beatles' first residency in Hamburg in late 1960, Stuart had decided to stay behind in Germany with Astrid Kirchherr, to whom he had become engaged. On 10 April 1962, however, he collapsed in Hamburg after suffering a brain haemorrhage. He passed away aged just 21 years and 10 months in Astrid's arms in the ambulance taking him to hospital.

ABOVE The house occupied in 1960 by Stuart Sutcliffe's family on Ullet Road near Sefton Park.

27. HUYTON PARISH CHURCH CEMETERY

Millie Sutcliffe arranged for her son's body to be returned to England for burial and his funeral was held on 19 April 1962. John, Paul, George and Pete Best were once again away for their latest Hamburg booking. Stuart's funeral was, however, attended by his girlfriend Astrid Kirchherr, The Beatles' Hamburg friend Klaus Voormann, John's girlfriend Cynthia, George's mum Louise, their early manager Allan Williams and his wife Beryl and Stuart's art college friend and flatmate Rod Murray.

LEFT Stuart Sutcliffe's grave in Huyton Parish Church cemetery, eight meals east of the city centre.

ABOVE Stuart Sutcliffe on bass as the band auditioned with stand-in drummer Johnny Hutchinson for impresario Larry Parnes in May 1960 at the Blue Angel Club, 106–108 Seel Street.

28. PENNY LANE

Penny Lane is a road in the Wavertree district of Liverpool running down towards Sefton Park. The famous Beatles' song that bears its name, however, references the bus (and one-time tram) terminus that stood at Penny Lane's junction with Smithdown Road and Allerton Road. Paul McCartney would have passed by Penny Lane when travelling to school at the Liverpool Institute or into the city.

The shelter in the middle of the roundabout at Penny Lane still exists and many of the other details in the song were also genuine locations. The barber's shop for example is believed to have been Bioletti's, which was located in the row of businesses by the roundabout. All The Beatles had their hair cut at Bioletti's at one time or another. Coincidentally hairdressers from the shop were employed to travel to the Salvation Army children's home up the road at Strawberry Field to cut the hair of the residents. The fire station mentioned in the song, however, would have been located a little further along the road to Allerton on Mather Avenue.

Paul recalled how he would often meet John at Penny Lane or change buses if he was travelling from his own home in Allerton to John's home in Woolton. Paul also remembers seeing a pretty nurse here selling British legion poppies from a tray. It was, of course, in October and November 1957, around the time of Remembrance Day, that Paul made his first appearances with The Quarrymen. Could this be the reason these images of Penny Lane stuck in his mind?

'Penny Lane' and 'Strawberry Fields Forever' were recorded in late 1966 and were two of the first numbers intended for *Sgt. Pepper's Lonely Hearts Club Band*. Instead of being included on the LP, however, they were released as a double A side single in February 1967, evoking a nostalgic recreation of John and Paul's childhood.

LEFT The junction of Penny Lane with Smithdown and Allerton Road, with the shelter in the middle of the roundabout visible in the background.

29. JOHN'S PRIMARY SCHOOLS

The first schools attended by John Lennon are on opposite sides of Penny Lane. John began at Mosspits School in Wavertree just over a month after his fifth birthday. At the time he and his mum Julia were living with her parents, George and Annie Stanley, at their terraced house on nearby Newcastle Road.

In March 1946, Julia took five-year-old John with her when she moved to a one-bedroom flat in Gateacre with her new partner Bobby Dykins. Julia's sister Mimi felt this situation was improper and so with the help of the Liverpool Public Assistance Committee, Julia was forced to give up her son and hand him over to Mimi's care. John moved in to live with Aunt Mimi and Uncle George at their house Mendips and was moved to a different primary school, Dovedale, located between the Penny Lane roundabout and Sefton Park.

ABOVE Mosspits and Dovedale Primary Schools attended by John Lennon; John aged six in his Dovedale school uniform.

30. 12 ARNOLD GROVE

George Harrison was born in a two-up two-down terraced house at 12 Arnold Grove, on 25 February 1943. His parents had rented this house soon after they married in 1931 while they waited to be allocated a council property. They had a long wait! They were finally given their council house in Speke in 1949!

LEFT George Harrison's birthplace and first home at Arnold Grove, Wavertree.

31. MENDIPS

251 Menlove Avenue, better known as Mendips, was the home of John Lennon's Aunt Mimi and her husband George Smith. George and Mimi moved here around the time the Second World War ended in 1945. They never had children of their own but a year after moving in, five-year-old John moved in with them.

John's bedroom was the upstairs room above the front door, while George and Mimi were next door above the living room. From 1947 the back bedroom was often rented out to veterinary students from Liverpool University, who would then treat Mimi's dog and cats for free! One early lodger at the house was a former sailor who played the harmonica. He taught John a couple of songs and John was presented with his harmonica as a Christmas present in 1947.

In June 1955, when John was 14, Uncle George suffered a haemorrhage and died the following day. Two years later John formed his band The Quarrymen but Mimi did not allow them to rehearse at Mendips. She was suspicious of Paul McCartney, who joined the group in late 1957, and even more so of George Harrison, who joined the following year. The boys nevertheless would visit John at Mendips and practise singing using the echo chamber effect that John claimed could be achieved in the front porch of the house.

John moved into a flat at Gambier Terrace with Stuart Sutcliffe during the time he was at Liverpool College of Art between 1959 and 1960. Subsequently he and his wife Cynthia moved into Brian Epstein's flat on Falkner Street after they married in August 1962.

BELOW John Lennon's childhood home Mendips on Menlove Avenue, Woolton, five miles south-east of Liverpool city centre.

32. MENLOVE AVENUE

Julia came to visit her sister Mimi at Mendips on 15 July 1958. Around 9.50pm she left Mendips and walked up Menlove Avenue with John's friend Nigel Walley, who had called by only to discover that John was not at home. At the next junction Nigel wished Julia goodnight and turned up Vale Road towards his own home. Julia then crossed Menlove Avenue to catch her bus back to Penny Lane and then on to her home in Allerton. Tragically she was run down before she reached the other side of the road. The site where John's mother was killed was just a minute's walk from Mendips and therefore clearly visible from the front gate.

When Nigel heard the sound of the accident behind him, he ran back to Mendips but Mimi had already heard the commotion outside. The car that hit Julia was driven by Eric Clague, a young off-duty policeman. An ambulance was called but Julia was declared dead on arrival at hospital. Clague was sent to trial but only received a reprimand and a period of suspension from duty. He nevertheless left the force and took a job as a postman instead. Among the streets to which he delivered mail was Forthlin Road. A few years after Julia's death, therefore, the man who ran her down was delivering hundreds of fan letters to Paul McCartney's home.

The couple moved back to Mendips following the birth of their son Julian in April 1963, by which time The Beatles were achieving fame and success and John was thus having to spend much of his time away.

In 1965, Mimi sold Mendips and John bought her a bungalow in Poole, Dorset where she lived until her death in 1991.

Mendips is open to the public, along with Paul's home at Forthlin Road, but visits to the two properties can only be arranged by booking in advance with the National Trust.

ABOVE John Lennon's bedroom at Mendips, restored by the National Trust to look as he would have known it, complete with posters of Elvis Presley and Brigitte Bardot.

RIGHT Julia Lennon was tragically killed a short distance from Mendips while crossing Menlove Avenue from the junction of Vale Road opposite.

33. STRAWBERRY FIELDS

Strawberry Fields was a gothic mansion built in the 1870s by Liverpool shipping magnate George Warren. The house appeared on an 1891 map with the name 'Strawberry Fields', although it subsequently became known as 'Strawberry Field'. It was later sold to another shipping merchant, Alexander C. Mitchell, after whose death his widow bequeathed the property to the Salvation Army. It was opened as an orphanage for girls in 1936 and by the 1950s boys were also being admitted.

The main entrance to Strawberry Fields on Beaconsfield Road is only a short walk along Menlove Avenue from John Lennon's childhood home Mendips. He is known to have come here with his Aunt Mimi to attend the summer fairs which were held in the grounds each year. More frequently, however, he would go round the corner into Vale Road where he could climb into the overgrown grounds of Strawberry Fields. Paul later described this area being like a wild secret area that was a hideaway, 'where

he could maybe have a smoke, live in his dreams… It was an escape for John'.

The original mansion was demolished in 1973 and a purpose-built children's home was later built on the site. John Lennon left money to the home in his will and in 1984 Yoko Ono, provided over £50,000 towards its upkeep. This home nevertheless closed in January 2005 but the site was opened to the public in 2019 with a new exhibition telling stories of the house and gardens and John's childhood. The original gates that stood at the entrance to Strawberry Fields are now located in the gardens.

The song 'Strawberry Fields Forever' was released in February 1967. A living memorial to John across a 2.5-acre site called Strawberry Fields in Central Park, New York and near his home at the Dakota Building, was opened on what would have been his 45th birthday on 9 October 1985.

BELOW The entrance to Strawberry Field as it once appeared. Today the site and gardens are open to the public with a visitor attraction telling the story of the old house and John Lennon's childhood.

34. VALE ROAD

John would climb over a wall round the corner from Mendips to access the overgrown grounds of Strawberry Fields, which in those days used to back on to Vale Road which runs behind Menlove Avenue. This access point to Strawberry Fields lay at a convenient spot as it was halfway between John's home and those of three of his great childhood friends.

Nigel Walley, Pete Shotton and Ivan Vaughan all lived along Vale Road. Ivan lived in the house directly behind Mendips. He had been at Dovedale Primary with John but for his secondary education his mother sent him to the Liverpool Institute in the city rather than Quarry Bank School with John, where she feared Lennon would distract him from his studies. At the Inny he befriended Paul McCartney, with whom he shared the same birthday and who he invited to the Woolton fete on 6 July 1957 and introduced to John.

A couple of doors along from Ivan lived Nigel Walley, who had been at Mosspits Primary with John and later went to the Bluecoat School near Penny Lane. Nigel was tea chest bass player with The Quarrymen before becoming their booking agent. It was Nigel who secured the band their first booking at The Cavern because he knew the owner's father as they were both members of the same golf club!

Further along Vale Road lived John's best friend Pete Shotton. Pete was washboard player in The Quarrymen. Pete was the one who bumped into Paul McCartney along Vale Road a couple of weeks after the Woolton fete and informed him that John wanted him to join The Quarrymen.

ABOVE The junction of Vale Road and Linkstor Road, Woolton, where Pete Shotton informed Paul McCartney that he had been invited to join The Quarrymen.

BELOW Calderstones Park lay between John Lennon's home on Menlove Avenue and his secondary school Quarry Bank.

35. CALDERSTONES PARK

John Lennon would have crossed Calderstones Park regularly on his way from his home on Menlove Avenue to his secondary school on Harthill Road. Paul also lived not far from the park in Allerton; when he unveiled the Linda McCartney Play Area in 1998, he recalled how he had played here as a child.

Also located in Calderstones Park is the Allerton Oak, which is believed to be the oldest oak tree in the north-west of England. The Calder Stones themselves are six megaliths from a Neolithic burial site which are now housed within a greenhouse in the park.

36. QUARRY BANK SCHOOL

On the edge of Calderstones Park was Quarry Bank High School for Boys (now Calderstones School) where John Lennon was a pupil between 1952 and 1957. Famously John did not do well academically at Quarry Bank or particularly enjoy his time there. He did, however, strive to keep his fellow pupils entertained with cartoons and funny stories which he jotted in an exercise book titled *The Daily Howl*.

It was also here, of course, that John formed his first band The Quarrymen, taking the group's name from the opening line of the school song: 'Quarrymen old before our birth...' John's inspiration was the skiffle music craze that had spread across the UK following Lonnie Donegan's 1956 hit single 'Rock Island Line'. The beauty of skiffle was that it made a virtue of cheaply available or even homemade instruments. John recruited Pete Shotton to play the quintessential skiffle instrument, the washboard, while fellow Quarry Bank pupils Eric Griffiths and Rod Davies contributed guitar and banjo respectively. A former pupil, Colin Hanton was the band's drummer. The job of tea chest bass player was filled by non-Quarry Bankers, first Nigel Walley, then Ivan Vaughan and then Len Garry (a friend of Ivan's from the Liverpool Institute).

The Quarrymen's performance at the Woolton fete on 6 July 1957 came at the end of John's final year at Quarry Bank. Around the same time, his headmaster Mr Pobjoy and English teacher, Mr Burnett, managed to get him on to a course at Liverpool College of Art, despite his poor exam results.

ABOVE Detention sheets revealing the school-day misdemeanours of a 15-year-old John Lennon, when he attended Quarry Bank School.

LEFT The entrance of the former Quarry Bank High School on Harthill Road, on the edge of Calderstones Park.

37. WOOLTON VILLAGE

The village of Woolton, like nearby Allerton and many other areas that now form the suburbs of Liverpool, is mentioned in the Domesday Book, King William I's 1086 survey of England and Wales 20 years after the Norman Conquest. To this day Woolton retains a village-like character all of its own, dominated by St Peter's Church and bordered by a golf course on one side and Woolton Woods on the other.

Woolton's stone quarries inspired the name of John Lennon's school, Quarry Bank as well as that of his band The Quarrymen. The Woolton quarries supplied 95 per cent of the stone used to build one of the greatest landmarks in Liverpool, the city's Anglican Cathedral. Architect Giles Gilbert Scott designed the building when he was 22 in 1904 and construction continued until his death in February 1960. By this time John Lennon and Stuart Sutcliffe were living in a student flat

in Gambier Terrace which directly overlooked the cathedral. Building work on the cathedral continued until 1978 and in the 1990s Woolton's southern quarry was developed for housing, although the sides of the old quarry remain visible.

ABOVE The centre of Woolton village, the area of Liverpool where John Lennon was brought up.

38. THE DAIRY COTTAGE

The Dairy Cottage in Woolton Village was once owned by John Lennon's Uncle George. John and his parents had initially lived at his grandparents' house in Wavertree but in 1942, George and his wife Mimi encouraged them to move into the Dairy Cottage. This became the only home that John and his two parents had to themselves. Their family life was, however, very brief as Alf had to return to sea with the merchant navy and Julia and John moved out of the Dairy Cottage in 1943.

LEFT The Dairy Cottage where John Lennon and his parents lived for a brief time from 1942.

LEFT St Peter's Church, Woolton, where John Lennon and Paul McCartney met on 6 July 1957.

39. ST PETER'S CHURCH

Building work began on St Peter's Church in Woolton in 1886. The church now stands on what is possibly the highest point in Liverpool. From the top of its tower it is possible to see not only Liverpool and Merseyside, but beyond to Lancashire, Cheshire and the Welsh hills.

It was the Woolton Parish Garden Fete held in the grounds of the church on 6 July 1957 that established St Peter's as a key place in music history.

The fete began with a procession of carnival floats at 2pm through the streets of the village, led by the brass band of the Cheshire Yeomanry. At the back end of the procession was a coal lorry, on the back of which sat John Lennon's band The Quarrymen. At first as the procession moved along, they attempted to play but eventually gave up and sat looking increasingly sullen. The formal opening of the fete at St Peter's Church followed at 3pm and then The Quarrymen began playing in a field at the back of the graveyard.

The Quarrymen's set began at around 4.15pm on a stage set up in the corner of the field and they played for about half an hour. Paul McCartney had cycled over from Allerton to meet his school friend Ivan Vaughan and recalled 'coming into the fete and seeing all the sideshows. And also hearing all this great music wafting in from this little Tannoy system. It was John and the band.'

John was singing the song 'Come Go With Me' by Pittsburgh doo-wop group The Del-Vikings, which had been a hit in the US. As John wasn't sure of all the words to the song, Paul recalled he had to improvise them. It was probably following this afternoon set in the church field that Ivan first introduced Lennon to McCartney.

40. ELEANOR RIGBY'S GRAVE

Among the graves in St Peter's churchyard is that for John's Uncle George, who had died in 1955. Coincidentally, another headstone here marks the grave of an Eleanor Rigby, who had lived locally and died on 10 October 1939, almost a year to the day before John's birth. Paul has, however, claimed that he had been unaware of the grave when he wrote the song 'Eleanor Rigby' for the 1996 Beatles album *Revolver*.

ABOVE The grave in which Eleanor Rigby is buried along with her grandparents John and Frances Rigby and their daughter Doris.

41. ST PETER'S CHURCH HALL

Following the afternoon fete, The Quarrymen played again for an evening dance beginning at 8pm in the church hall just across the road. While they waited, Paul borrowed John's guitar and used it to play a few numbers including 'Twenty Flight Rock' and 'Be Bop a Lula'. Paul would, of course, have had to play John's guitar upside down and strung the wrong way round for a lefthander like himself. Nevertheless his performance on guitar and then on the church hall piano on which he played 'Long Tall Sally' and 'Whole Lotta Shakin'' must have been impressive as it secured him an invitation a few weeks later to join The Quarrymen. He remembered John leaning over 'with his beery breath' and joining in as he played the piano. It was therefore in St Peter's Church Hall that John and Paul first played music together.

ABOVE St Peter's Church Hall, where The Quarrymen played in the evening following the Woolton fete on 6 July 1957.

42. 20 FORTHLIN ROAD

By the time they moved to Forthlin Road in Allerton, Paul McCartney and his family had lived at a series of addresses across Merseyside. As a newborn in 1942, Paul's first home had been at Sunbury Road, Anfield. The family then moved to a house in Wallasey, Wirral, next to a prefab home in Knowsley and then to a flat in Everton. In 1947 they moved to Western Avenue in Speke and then three years later to Ardwick Road in the same area.

Paul, Mike and their parents Jim and Mary finally arrived in Forthlin Road in April 1956. The house was then four years old and the rent was £1 19s 10d a week. Paul's bedroom was the small room at the front of the house above the front door, while his parents were in the larger front bedroom next door. Mike had the bedroom at the back. Tragically it was only a few months after moving here that Paul's mother Mary began to develop symptoms of breast cancer. She had a mastectomy but the disease had already spread. She was taken to hospital suffering from a brain tumour and died on 31 October 1956.

George Harrison would visit Paul at Forthlin Road and play guitar in the front downstairs room while Paul played the trumpet, this being the instrument Paul's dad had bought him for his 13th birthday. Jim McCartney was a trumpeter himself and had led Jim Mac's Band in the 1920s. Paul traded in his trumpet to buy himself a guitar in July 1957, soon after his meeting with John Lennon at the Woolton fete.

John Lennon began visiting Paul at Forthlin Road and it was here they started to compose songs together, or as they called them their 'Lennon-McCartney originals'. The songs that Paul wrote or began to write here included 'Love Me Do', 'Michelle', 'Like Dreamers Do', 'I'll Follow The Sun' and 'Love of the Loved'.

The house was used for Quarrymen rehearsal sessions in 1958; in 1960 the group,

OPPOSITE George, John and Paul photographed by Paul's brother Mike at the back door of 20 Forthlin Road in October 1962.

LEFT Paul McCartney's home at 20 Forthlin Road, Allerton.

by then known as The Beatles, recorded themselves here using a Grundig reel-to-reel tape recorder.

Mike McCartney took many famous photographs of his brother and his bandmates here, including a 1962 shot of Paul playing guitar in the back garden, which was used for the cover of the 2005 album *Chaos and Creation In The Backyard*. Paul officially moved from this house to live in London in 1964. Later that same year he bought his dad a much larger home in Gayton, Wirral, so enabling the McCartney family's final departure from Liverpool.

The house at 20 Forthlin Road, like Mendips, is open to the public but visits to the two properties can only be arranged by booking in advance with the National Trust.

43. BLOMFIELD ROAD

A few minutes' walk from Paul's house Is Blomfield Road, where John Lennon's mother Julia and her partner John 'Bobby' Dykins lived. Although he had been brought up by his Aunt Mimi and Uncle George from the age of five, John began reconnecting with his mother and visiting her here from 1951. It was here that Julia taught her son to play the piano and banjo. Later Paul and other members of The Quarrymen would come here to practise.

44. ALLERTON CEMETERY

John's mum Julia Lennon is buried in Allerton Cemetery. Her funeral service was held on 21 July and John is said to have cried all the way through it.

Also buried in Allerton Cemetery are other Liverpool legends, including singer, presenter and friend of The Beatles Cilla Black, and Ken Dodd, one of the city's most famous comedians, who appeared on several occasions with the band on stage and television.

FAR LEFT The home on Blomfield Road, Allerton, where Julia Lennon lived with her partner Bobby Dykins and their children Julia and Jackie.

LEFT The grave of Julia Lennon in Allerton Cemetery is marked with a simple stone listing her as 'Mummy', together with the names of her children.

45. SPEKE

The Liverpool suburb of Speke lies around eight miles south-east of the city centre. It was once a small and ancient village but the housing estate that now dominates Speke was constructed as a self-contained satellite town by Liverpool Corporation from the 1930s to address the problem of poor housing in the city.

The McCartney family moved to a then brand-new house at 72 Western Avenue, Speke in August 1947, when Paul was five and his brother Mike was three. It was the first house that Paul could remember and when he moved here he recalled the road outside was still being built, the roadside grass being sown and trees planted. The McCartneys got their home rent free because Paul's mother Mary had taken a job as resident midwife for the surrounding estate. They stayed for three years until 1950, when Mary changed jobs to become a health visitor.

The McCartneys' next home was 12 Ardwick Road, which Paul recalled as being 'really unfinished' when they moved in and they had to slop through mud for the first year they were here. Jim McCartney was a keen gardener and is said to have grown dahlias, snapdragons and a lavender hedge in the

ABOVE Aerial view over Speke and the surrounding countryside on the banks of the Mersey, which Paul loved to explore as a boy.

front garden and to have sent his sons out to collect horse manure for use as fertiliser. Aged eight when he moved here, Paul developed his love of nature by exploring the countryside beyond the estate. Paul would cycle out to the side of the Mersey and along to nearby Hale Head Lighthouse. In 1956, the McCartneys moved yet again, this time to perhaps their most famous address at Forthlin Road in Allerton.

A third Beatle house in Speke lies at 25 Upton Green, another then new home to which George Harrison's family moved when he was aged six in 1949. This is, therefore, where George was living in the 1950s when he would catch the bus into the city to go to school at the Liverpool Institute. It was, of course, on that bus journey that he met Paul McCartney, and it was these meetings that led to his being asked to join John and Paul in The Quarrymen.

46. LIVERPOOL JOHN LENNON AIRPORT

Speke Airport was first established in 1930 and developed to become a major international airport after the Second World War. In 2001 it was renamed Liverpool John Lennon Airport in honour of the Beatle, 21 years after his murder. The *Yellow Submarine* artwork was moved here to welcome visitors in 2005, having originally been created for the Liverpool International Garden Festival in 1984.

ABOVE Liverpool John Lennon Airport, complete with *Yellow Submarine*.

47. SPEKE HALL

The airport was constructed on part of the grounds of Speke Hall. An earlier Speke Hall is mentioned as far back as the Domesday Book in 1086. The current building, however, is a magnificent half-timbered mansion built by Sir William Norris in 1530 during the reign of Henry VIII. This house still stands and is now owned by the National Trust and open to visitors.

RIGHT Speke Hall, a magnificent Tudor mansion next to Liverpool John Lennon Airport.

48. NEW CLUBMOOR HALL

John's friend Nigel Walley arranged for The Quarrymen to play for events held by the local Conservative club at the New Clubmoor Hall five miles out from the city centre. The Quarrymen's first appearance at this rather drab looking venue was on Friday 18 October, but nevertheless proved to be a historic occasion as it was Paul McCartney's debut with the band.

Paul said he had joined as the group's lead guitarist but when he had to do a solo on the song 'Guitar Boogie' he had 'sticky fingers'. 'I just blew it!' he recalled. 'I couldn't play at all and I got terribly embarrassed!' Charlie McBain, the promoter who had booked the shows, wrote on the back of their business card 'Good & Bad'. The famous photo of John and Paul in matching ties and jackets leading the band was taken on their second appearance at this venue on 23 November 1957.

ABOVE The New Clubmoor Hall, where on Friday 18 October 1957 Paul McCartney made his debut on stage alongside John Lennon.

BELOW Paul and John fronting The Quarrymen at the New Clubmoor Hall on 23 November 1957, a month after Paul had made his debut with the band at the same venue.

49. THE CASBAH

The Casbah was the club run by Beatles drummer Pete Best's mother Mona in the basement of their home. According to family legend, Mona Best bought 8 Hayman's Green with funds acquired after pawning her jewellery and betting the proceeds on a horse ridden by Lester Piggott in the 1954 Epsom Derby. Mona and her sons Pete and Rory moved into the house in 1957. Mona then opened the Casbah Club in the basement of the property in 1959, hosting live bands and serving coffee and Coca-Cola to local teenagers. The Quarrymen played here on numerous occasions from the club's opening night.

In August 1960, The Beatles (as they were by then known) recruited Mona's son Pete as their drummer for their forthcoming bookings in Hamburg, Germany. Pete's friend Neil Aspinall (a former classmate of Paul McCartney at the Liverpool Institute) became the band's roadie. At the same time Neil became a lodger at the Bests' home. The van used to ferry The Beatles around would have been parked outside the house at the end of each day and the band's amps and equipment stored in the hallway. Also around the same time Neil began a relationship with Mona, who at 36 was literally twice his age.

The Beatles played their last show at the Casbah in June 1962, just a few weeks after their first recording session with George Martin at EMI's Abbey Road recording studio in London. The club was closed down at the end of that month following a death in the Best family, while the session with George Martin ultimately led to Pete's dismissal from the band in August. By this time Mona was pregnant by Neil Aspinall and their son Roag was born on 31 August 1962. Despite the difficult situation, Neil remained roadie to The Beatles as well as continuing to lodge with the Bests for some time after.

ABOVE The Casbah Club was based in the basement of Mona Best's West Derby home, around five miles north-east of Liverpool city centre.

50. LOWLANDS

Just along Hayman's Green from the Casbah is Lowlands, a prestigious Victorian house which in the 1950s came into the possession of the West Derby Community Association. In 1958 the basement was opened as a youth centre, which hosted a weekly club featuring local bands. One of the groups who regularly played here was the Les Stewart Quartet, of which George Harrison was a member even though he was also a Quarryman. Mona Best asked the Les Stewart Quartet to play on the opening night of The Casbah on Saturday 29 August 1959, but unfortunately Les and his band fell out with one another. George called in the services of his friends John and Paul and so The Quarrymen fulfilled the booking instead.

ABOVE Lowlands stands just along the road from the Casbah.

51. NEW BRIGHTON TOWER BALLROOM

The Tower Ballroom in New Brighton, Wirral was one of the Merseyside venues The Beatles played most often during their early career. Sadly the building no longer stands having been destroyed by fire in April 1969. The ballroom had, however, long outlived New Brighton Tower from which it took its name. This had stood over it from the time of its construction in 1894 to its being dismantled in 1919. New Brighton Tower had been influenced by the Eiffel Tower and, at 567 feet, was even taller than the 518-foot Blackpool Tower up the coast in Lancashire.

The Beatles first played at the Tower Ballroom in November 1961 as part of a presentation named Operation Big Beat. This was a package featuring a number of local groups including Gerry and the Pacemakers, the Remo Four, Kingsize Taylor and the Dominoes and Rory Storm and the Hurricanes, whose drummer at the time was, of course, Ringo Starr. Interestingly, NEMS were named

as a ticket outlet for this performance, before Brian Epstein claimed he had first heard about The Beatles.

The Beatles played here regularly over the next year including 17 August 1962, the day after Pete Best's dismissal from the band when Johnny Hutchinson sat in as drummer.

Another significant show for The Beatles at New Brighton came on Friday 12 October 1962, just after the release of 'Love Me Do', when they played on a bill with one of their rock and roll heroes Little Richard. The Beatles also made an important new friend that night in Little Richard's keyboard player, Billy Preston, who would work with them during the *Let It Be* sessions in early 1969. The band's final appearance at the Tower Ballroom was on 14 June 1963, by which time they had scored their first UK number one single with 'From Me To You'.

ABOVE The view across the Mersey to Liverpool from a point adjacent to the former site of New Brighton's Tower Ballroom.

52. LITHERLAND TOWN HALL

Litherland is an area lying close to the docklands north of Liverpool city centre. In late 1960 and through 1961, the area provided the venue for a number of Beatles live shows including one of the most significant in their career. The Beatles played at Litherland Town Hall on 27 December 1960, a few weeks after they returned from their first residency in Hamburg. This show has been noted as a turning point in their career perhaps not least because of the improvement in their performance that had occurred during their two months playing each night on the Reeperbahn. The Beatles' line-up that night was surprising, however, as it included not only John, Paul, George and Pete Best, but also Pete's friend Chas Newby on bass standing in for Stuart Sutcliffe, who had stayed behind in Germany.

The band was introduced on stage by Cavern DJ Bob Wooler. They began playing as soon as they heard their names at which point the curtains drew back to reveal them belting out 'Long Tall Sally'. Adverts for the show described the band as being 'direct from Hamburg' which famously led some to assume they were German. The show nevertheless went down a storm with the Litherland audience and led to multiple new offers of bookings for the coming year of 1961.

ABOVE New Brighton's Tower Ballroom as The Beatles would have known it in the early 1960s.

LEFT The Beatles played at the Tower Ballroom on 27 occasions, including this in July 1962, headlined by Joe Brown, who would become a great friend of George Harrison.

RIGHT Litherland Town Hall, where The Beatles played over 20 times in 1960 and 1961.

53. GROSVENOR BALLROOM

In the early 1960s the Grosvenor Ballroom in the Liscard area of Wallasey was said to be a rough venue where rival gangs of teddy boys from Birkenhead and Wallasey would congregate and threaten violence both to one another and to visiting bands. The Beatles played here on 14 occasions and with no less than five different drummers. Their first appearance here was in June 1960 when their drummer was Tommy Moore, who at 36 was more than twice George's age.

When they arrived for a booking at the Grosvenor on 11 June 1960, The Beatles discovered Tommy had left them for a job at Garston bottle works. They therefore took to the stage with no drummer and John began the show by asking if anyone in the audience fancied sitting in for the night. Trouble ensued when a rough tough teddy boy known as Ronnie volunteered despite having never played drums before in his life. Ronnie spent the evening thrashing away before announcing that he intended to continue as their permanent drummer.

The Beatles played the Grosvenor again with their next official drummer Norman Chapman, who was forced to leave a few weeks later when he was called up for National Service. Grosvenor audiences next saw The Beatles with Paul McCartney having to act as the band's drummer. By the time of their last appearances at the Grosvenor the band had become the more recognisable line-up of John, Paul, George and Pete Best.

ABOVE Wallasey's Grosvenor Ballroom, where The Beatles played regularly between June 1960 and September 1961.

ABOVE The former site of Albert Marrion's photography studio in Wallasey Village.

54. 268 WALLASEY VILLAGE

This shop was once the premises of Albert Marrion's photographers. In December 1961, The Beatles' newly appointed manager Brian Epstein sent them to Marrion for their first ever official photo session. The resulting image taken on these premises showed John, Paul, George and Pete Best in their leather outfits and is one of the best known early photos of the band. It famously appeared on the front cover of the *Mersey Beat* newspaper dated 4 January 1962, under the headline 'Beatles Top Poll!'

55. NESTON INSTITUTE

The Beatles played in Neston, a small Wirral market town some distance from their Liverpool homes, on Thursday 2 June 1960. The show is of historic interest because of the review that followed in local paper, *The Heswall and Neston Advertiser*, which described them as 'Liverpool Rhythm group "The Beatles"'. This is believed to be the first time that the band's name appeared in print.

ABOVE The Neston Institute, where The Beatles played in June 1960, is today the town's Civic Hall.

RIGHT John Lennon teased his girlfriend Cynthia for coming from the genteel Wirral but her home on Trinity Road, Hoylake, was more modest than his at Mendips.

56. TRINITY ROAD

Before her marriage to John Lennon, Cynthia Powell lived on Trinity Road, Hoylake, Wirral with her family. Following her father's death in 1956, her mother rented out a room here so Cynthia could afford to attend Liverpool College of Art. Cynthia moved back to Trinity Road with her baby Julian in late 1963 when The Beatles had achieved fame across the UK. When she had Julian christened in the Hoylake Parish Church which then stood almost opposite the house, the event was photographed and featured in British national newspapers, thereby breaking the secret of John's marriage.

RIGHT John Lennon with his first wife Cynthia at the height of The Beatles' success.

57. HULME HALL

Port Sunlight is a Wirral village created in the late 19th century by the manufacturer of Sunlight Soap, William Lever (later Lord Leverhulme), to provide homes for his workers. Port Sunlight's public buildings included Gladstone Hall, named after Prime Minister William Gladstone, and Hulme Hall, named in honour of Lever's wife Elizabeth Hulme.

The Beatles were booked to play here on 18 August 1962 for an event arranged by the local horticultural society. They had recently dismissed their drummer Pete Best and so it was that the members of the Port Sunlight horticultural society were the first to witness a performance by the band's new official line-up of John, Paul, George and Ringo.

The Beatles appeared here four times during 1962. Before taking to the stage for their final visit on 27 October, they recorded their earliest surviving broadcast interview for the nearby Clatterbridge and Cleaver Hospitals' radio service. The chat catches the band at a fascinating moment before the phenomenal rise to fame which would occur over the next year. They discuss their recently issued first single 'Love Me Do'; Ringo, who only joined the band nine weeks earlier, mentions their forthcoming final residency in Hamburg in December; and John talks about the work they need to do on their next single, which would be 'Please Please Me', released in January 1963.

BELOW Hulme Hall, Port Sunlight, where in August 1962 The Beatles made their debut with their new official line-up with Ringo on drums.